THE ADVENTURES OF SUPERMAN™

BY
PATRICIA RELF

ILLUSTRATED BY
KURT SCHAFFENBERGER
AND DAVID HUNT

A GOLDEN BOOK, New York
Western Publishing Company, Inc.
Racine, Wisconsin 53404

Long ago, on the planet Krypton, a scientist named Jor-El made a frightening discovery. "Our planet is going to explode soon!" he told his wife. "Everything will be destroyed. We must try to save our baby son."

Jor-El built a small rocket ship for the baby. "We will send our son far away to a planet called Earth," he told his wife. "There he will be safe."

They kissed their baby good-by, put him into the rocket ship, and sadly watched it take off.

For two years the baby flew through space, safe inside his little rocket ship.

When the rocket ship landed on Earth, a farmer and his wife, driving along in their truck, saw the ship at the side of the road. They were amazed to find a little boy inside.

JUMPING JEHOSHOPHAT!

Ma and Pa Kent adopted the child as their own son. They named him Clark. It wasn't long before they realized that Clark was a very unusual boy. For one thing—he could fly!

Clark was also very strong.

Fortunately, Clark's hair did not grow long—for no scissors could cut

Clark could see things that were very far away.

Clark could run faster than the eye could see.

His heat vision was red hot! And he could see through everything but lead.

Clark's clothes wore out almost as quickly as Ma Kent made them. Ordinary cloth just wasn't strong enough for a boy with super powers. Ma Kent made a super suit for him to wear under his clothes. She used the yarn from the super-strong blankets that she had found in the little rocket ship. Nothing could harm Clark's special suit—and it stretched as he grew!

When Clark started going to school, Pa Kent had a talk with him.

"Your special powers could frighten people, Clark," he said, "so you must try to hide them. When the time comes, you should use your powers to help people."

Many years passed and Clark grew up.
He became a news reporter.

And he never forgot his father's advice. He used his amazing
super powers to fight crime and help people everywhere.

One day Clark and his friend Lois Lane were watching a news
film on television.

"Too bad you're not as strong as *he* is, Clark," Lois said.
No one—not even Lois Lane—suspected that shy, meek
Clark Kent was really . . . Superman!

One morning in the news room,
Clark heard a voice from far away. . . .

He rushed to a nearby storeroom
and tore off his business suit.

Faster than a jet plane,
Superman flew over the city.

With his super vision he
scanned the streets below.

Outside, the other two robbers' backpacks opened up. Whirling blades popped out and the two crooks took off into the air. One of them switched on a two-way radio. "McGee to base," he said. "Dodge has been caught! Weems and I are on our way in."

The radio crackled. "Base to McGee. As long as *you've* got the money! Report in five minutes. Over and out."

With super speed, Superman
flew after the escaping robbers.
He grabbed the spinning
blades of the crooks' flying
machines. The blades stopped
spinning. . . .

But now the two *crooks*
whirled around and around.
The bank's money flew
everywhere.

Superman tucked the crooks safely under one arm
and spread his cape. In an instant, he had caught
all the falling money before it hit the ground.

Then Superman took the money and the crooks to the police.
Suddenly a voice came over the crooks' radio. "Come in,
McGee. Where are you? Is anything wrong? Report at once!"
Superman grabbed the radio.

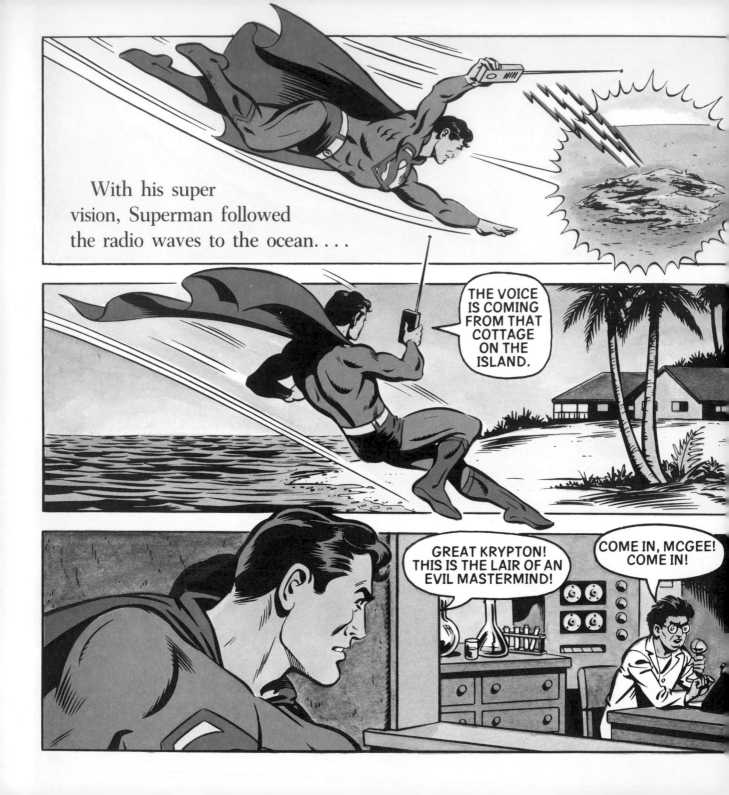

As the boat left,
a switch automatically
set off a bomb.

But of course the explosion didn't hurt Superman. He sped through the water like a torpedo, lifted up the crook's boat, and carried it back to shore.

"Well, it looks as if you've wrapped up the whole gang, Superman," the police chief said as he locked the last of the criminals in jail. "For all the people of Metropolis, I thank you."

Back in the news room, Lois Lane read Clark's news story about the bank robbery.

"This is a pretty exciting story, Clark," she said. "I'd give anything to know who that Superman *really* is!"

Clark Kent just smiled—and winked an eye.